TWELVE YEARS AND THIRTEEN DAYS

A portion of the proceeds from the sale of this book benefits Wellstone Action!,
a nonprofit organization dedicated to continuing Paul and Sheila Wellstone's fight for progressive change and economic justice.

For more information, write to Wellstone Action!, 821 Raymond Avenue, Suite 260, St. Paul, Minnesota 55114 or visit www.wellstone.org.

TWELVE YEARS AND THIRTEEN DAYS

# Remembering Paul and Sheila Wellstone

TERRY GYDESEN

**ESSAY BY JEFF BLODGETT**

FOREWORD BY WALTER F. MONDALE

UNIVERSITY OF MINNESOTA PRESS

Minneapolis · London

For David and Mark Wellstone,
and for Paul and Sheila's grandchildren,
Cari, Keith, Joshua, Matt, Acacia, and Sidney

The University of Minnesota Press
gratefully acknowledges a gift
from the Samuel and Sylvia Kaplan Fund
of The Minneapolis Foundation
to help support the publication of this book.

Library of Congress Cataloging-in-Publication Data

Gydesen, Terry.
Twelve years and thirteen days:
remembering Paul and Sheila Wellstone / Terry Gydesen;
essay by Jeff Blodgett; foreword by Walter F. Mondale.
p. cm.
ISBN 0-8166-4428-4 (PB : alk. paper)
1. Wellstone, Paul David (1944–2002)—Pictorial works.
2. Wellstone, Sheila, d. 2002—Pictorial works.
3. Legislators—United States—Pictorial works.
4. Legislators' spouses—United States—Pictorial works.
I. Title.
E840.8.W47 G93 2003
328.73'092'2—dc21
                                2003014293

Frontispiece: Paul and Sheila Wellstone, 1996

Photographs copyright 2003 by Terry Gydesen

"Portraits of a Passionate Man"
copyright 2003 by Jeff Blodgett

Foreword copyright 2003 by Walter F. Mondale

Published by the University of Minnesota Press
111 Third Avenue South, Suite 290
Minneapolis, MN 55401-2520
http://www.upress.umn.edu

Printed in the United States of America on acid-free paper

Design by Jeanne Lee

The University of Minnesota is an equal-opportunity
educator and employer.

12 11 10 09 08 07 06 05 04 03

10 9 8 7 6 5 4 3 2 1

The future will belong to those
who have passion,
and to those who are willing
to make the personal commitment
to make our country better.

**PAUL WELLSTONE**

# CONTENTS

# Foreword

**WALTER F. MONDALE**

Paul Wellstone was one of the most valiant public servants I have ever known, and he and his wife Sheila were among the most impressive public couples in America. Paul considered Sheila to be his cosenator and they fought to change this country and affirm the democratic ideals that we cherish. Together, they touched countless lives.

Paul came seemingly out of nowhere to defeat a well-funded incumbent senator in 1990, but his victory was not a fluke: he built a winning campaign by encouraging thousands of Minnesotans to organize and become involved in the political process to demand a government that truly served them. Minnesotans voted for Paul because they knew his concern for them was genuine and he truly would represent "the little guy" in Washington.

During his twelve years as a U.S. senator, Paul championed the causes of working men and women, family farmers, seniors, children living in poverty, and veterans. He worked to maintain and strengthen environmental protections. He resisted efforts to privatize Social Security. He fought for affordable prescription drugs for seniors and decent health care for everyone. He collaborated with Republican members of the Senate to pass legislation mandating that mental health care be covered by Medicare and insurance providers. Sheila was a tireless advocate for victims of domestic violence and, with Paul, coauthored the first Violence Against Women Act in 1994.

A few weeks before Election Day in 2002, when Paul was again locked in a tough reelection campaign, I asked him, "Paul, are you going to win this election? What do the polls say?" And he said, "Never mind the polls. I've got a secret weapon that they don't know about. I've got the best kids that any candidate ever had in a campaign, and on Election Day they will show us how to win." Paul had proven twice before that grassroots politics is a winning politics, and I think all Minnesotans knew that Paul was going to win that election.

When his plane went down on the morning of October 25, it was as if the world had been suddenly turned upside down. While we grieved over such an enormous loss, we knew that Paul would want us to carry on the fight. I was deeply honored when David and Mark Wellstone asked me to take their father's place on the ballot even though to begin a political campaign at one of the saddest moments in Minnesota history felt almost unseemly. Yet someone had to carry Paul's torch and make certain that this tragedy did not end in futility.

We kept the faith and fought the good fight. I am very proud of the campaign that we ran and proud of all of the volunteers and staff who regrouped and gave all that they had. I know Paul would have been proud, too. On the morning after the election, I told the many young people who worked so hard on the campaign that one's ideals are often tested more in defeat than in victory. This was not the end but the beginning of what they could do for our state. More than anything, Paul would want us all to stand up and keep fighting.

Terry Gydesen spent many hours on the campaign trail in Paul's now-famous green bus. She photographed Paul greeting people on the street and in cafés, speaking at political rallies at union halls and colleges, encouraging his campaign volunteers, and celebrating his remarkable victories with his family, friends, and supporters. Terry captured the infectious enthusiasm, spontaneous joy, and boundless energy that Paul brought to doing what he loved best: meeting people, laughing and crying with them, listening to their concerns, and striving to earn their trust as their public servant.

When Terry learned of the plane accident she immediately went to the Wellstone campaign office in St. Paul. She photographed the stunned reaction of campaign staff, volunteers, and supporters who gathered there. She poignantly captured the grief and outpouring of affection for Paul and Sheila, which was especially evident in the impromptu shrine that grew along University Avenue day by day outside the office. Terry traveled with Joan and me just as she had with Paul and Sheila, documenting our remarkable and brief campaign as we endeavored to succeed our martyred senator. When it became apparent that we had not won, Terry was also there to capture our disappointment.

Paul and Sheila Wellstone will live long in the memory of Minnesotans and people throughout the world who share their commitment to democracy. May this simple and elegant book of photographs help keep their memory alive and inspire us to be the active trustees of their legacy of social justice and decency.

# Preface

Politics is what we create by what we do,
what we hope for,
and what we dare to imagine.

**PAUL WELLSTONE**

In 1990, a friend who is active in the Minnesota Democratic-Farmer-Labor Party (DFL) suggested, "You should follow Paul Wellstone's campaign. You'll probably like him, but he doesn't stand a chance of winning." That was the conventional wisdom. He didn't have enough money to be a serious threat to the incumbent Rudy Boschwitz, who had amassed a six-million-dollar campaign-fund war chest.

My passion for documenting political campaigns began in 1988 when I became Jesse Jackson's staff photographer. I was still a photography student at the time, so it was a big break for me and a rare opportunity to be on the inside of a national political campaign. The hope and passion of his Rainbow Coalition inspired me and I found myself drawn to politics.

Many of the people I knew on the Jackson campaign then went to work for this guy named Paul Wellstone. He was a small man with big ideas. He had a passionate staff of campaign workers, many of whom had been his students at Carleton College. This was the ultimate real-life political science lesson: the college professor putting into practice what he had been teaching for years about how to build a grassroots organization.

One of my first trips with Paul was on a small plane up to Duluth and Hibbing. At the beginning of a project, there is often one key image that inspires an entire body of work, and I made one such photograph on that trip. For me, the photograph taken at the Duluth Senior Center represents the hope that here was a politician who would stand up and fight for average people. Most politicians enter a room and shake hands; Paul gave hugs. He had a unique impact on people and seemed to gain their trust immediately.

I continued documenting what I have come to call the politics of passion and began an examination of extremes in American electoral politics. During the 1992 presidential campaign, I followed Pat Buchanan and Jerry

Paul and Sheila with State Representative Scott Dibble and State Representative Karen Clark
**Loring Park, Minneapolis, 2002**

Brown. Their political philosophies contrasted sharply, but their supporters shared an equal level of passion. Early in 1996 I traveled to New Hampshire and Iowa, photographing the presidential primaries. I spent the majority of my time again following Pat Buchanan and the religious right wing of the Republican Party. My photographs were political satire, and as I listened to their rhetoric I found myself growing angry and cynical.

That same year, Paul was beginning a tough reelection campaign in a rematch against Boschwitz. The race had become particularly nasty as the Republicans spent millions on attack ads. I photographed the state DFL convention where Paul won the party's endorsement. For the first time I felt great disappointment with Paul because he had just announced that he was voting for the Defense of Marriage Act. I didn't learn until after his death that in recent years he said that this was one vote he felt he had cast incorrectly.

Throughout the summer of 1996 I followed Paul when I was in the Twin Cities. I hadn't spent much time on his famous green bus in 1990, and I focused on it during the 1996 campaign. It had become a potent symbol. While his opponent spent millions on his campaign, Paul traveled the state in his refurbished old school bus complete with speaking platform on the back, delivering his populist message and building grassroots support. The bus came to

represent Paul—a man with no pretense who was fair and honest, who worked hard, and who got the job done. My focus on the bus culminated in a triumphant photograph of Paul, Sheila, and their daughter Marcia stepping off the bus as they arrived at the victory celebration on election night.

In 1996 I also went to the Republican National Convention in San Diego, where I realized that spending time in such a hateful political environment was taking an emotional toll on me. Pat Buchanan was blaming feminists, the media, and, most of all, homosexuals for seemingly all the ills of the world. I fall into all three categories so it was frightening to hear the cheers of the crowd surrounding me on the convention floor. After a couple more years I became burned out on politics and decided to pursue other projects.

The last time I saw Paul and Sheila was during the summer of 2002 at a rally in Loring Park in Minneapolis. My friend Scott Dibble was running for state senate and needed photos with Paul for a campaign brochure. I hadn't seen Paul and Sheila for at least two years, and I was greeted with big hugs from both of them. What I most remember from that day was Sheila's speech; I had heard her speak many times before, but I was very struck by how much more powerful and eloquent she had become. The Wellstones really were an amazing, loving team. I was inspired and considered returning to the campaign trail, but I was too busy with other commitments that now seem very unimportant.

On October 3, 2002, Paul moved me once again with his stance against an unprecedented preemptive strike policy and U.S. action alone against Iraq. This speech showed Paul at his best. He took a controversial stand even though he was in a very tight race for a third term in the Senate. I had a job out of state at that time, but I had planned to return to Minnesota to document the final week of his campaign. I was going to send Paul an e-mail message praising his speech, but decided to wait and tell him in person when I saw him. I was certain I would be photographing his victory party once again.

On the morning of October 25, I was finishing my client's work before going to the campaign office to get his schedule. When I first heard the news of the plane crash, I prayed that Sheila was not on board, too. Moments later came the news that not only Sheila but also Marcia and three staff people were on the plane. I immediately rushed to the campaign office and spent the next thirteen days documenting this very sad time in Minnesota's history.

Throughout those thirteen days I kept thinking about Paul's first Senate race and how Paul and Sheila had inspired so many people. Photographs I had taken of them over the years flashed through my mind. I watched his amazing staff switch from planning rallies and fund-raisers to organizing memorial services and funerals, then flip back to campaign mode to help Walter Mondale with his brief campaign. The shock and grief were too much to bear. Like the staff and volunteers, I worked to keep myself busy. This experience was an epiphany. My passion for politics returned.

Through the deaths of Paul and Sheila, I recognized the importance of involvement. In his book *The Conscience of a Liberal*, Paul wrote: "The future will not belong to those who are cynical or those who stand on the sidelines. The future will belong to those who have passion and are willing to work hard to make our country better." My new project is to work with the leaders who are continuing the Wellstone tradition of building strong and diverse coalitions and reaching out to people who have not previously been involved in politics.

I offer my photographs as a tribute to the work and leadership of the Wellstones. I will miss their voices fighting for peace and social justice, and I will really miss those hugs.

*Minneapolis*
*June 2003*

# Acknowledgments

There are many people to thank, and first and foremost is Todd Orjala and the staff of the University of Minnesota Press for believing so strongly in this project. I am honored that my book now stands alongside Paul's three books published by the Press.

I also wish to thank the following people: Jeff Blodgett for working with me on this book and adding his words and insight about the past twelve years and these amazing campaigns. Walter Mondale for stepping forward; I am sorry his voice of diplomacy and reason is not representing us in Washington. Mary Virginia Swanson for her guidance and insight into book publishing. Marcia Avner for the years of support and for providing the first arms that held me on October 25, 2002—and for whispering in my ear as I cried on her shoulder, "You do your thing and create a record of this time." Scott Adams and Kris Blake for welcoming me those early days in 1990 and being among the campfire group who decided Paul was the one who could beat Rudy Boschwitz. Scott Dibble for needing campaign photos last year so I have at least one recent memory of Paul and Sheila from 2002. Dick Senese for obtaining a press credential for me the night of Walter Mondale's historic nomination, and Bill Harper for getting me backstage that night. Cory Barton for getting my new Web site up and running so quickly. Keri Pickett and Michal Daniel for all the great editing help and for the inspiration they give me with their work. Ann Marsden for being a great teacher, mentor, and friend, and for pushing me to believe in myself during those early years. Petronella Ytsma for feeding my body and soul with her love and support. My good friend Margaret Stenger for the great food and for making my opening show of these photographs the best party ever, and Fay Miller and Ellen Richman for hanging the show. Janet, Bernel, and Ruby Bayliss for their love and support through a most difficult time of my life.

I especially thank the Wellstone staff and volunteers who allowed me into their lives during those awful thirteen days. Thank you, Jim Farrell, for granting me access to the office. To Allison Dobson, Kelly Bjorklund, Aaron Levy, Bill Lofy, Rick Kahn, Pam Wetterlund, C. Scott Cooper, and everyone at Grassroots Solutions, I treasure our new friendships that have developed.

The biggest thank-you goes to Paul, Sheila, Marcia, Mary, Will, and Tom. Your leadership will be missed but never forgotten.

Paul hugs Jeff Blodgett on election night, 1996

# Portraits of a Passionate Man

**JEFF BLODGETT**

Over the weekend of February 28 and March 1, 2003, four months after Paul and Sheila Wellstone died, a symposium was held at Carleton College that examined their lives and their impact on state and national politics. Paul would have loved it—an overflow crowd of former students and staff, political admirers, and people who had never met him showed up to talk about progressive politics and the Wellstone legacy. At one of the forums, someone asked whether Paul Wellstone's success as a political leader and his ability to win and hold high political office was the result of his own personal charisma or a model that could be employed by other populists and progressives.

The answer is both. Paul Wellstone had an unmatched capacity to inspire and motivate people across the country to act on their convictions, because he himself had the courage to do so in his own life. He was an electrifying speaker and articulate spokesman, and few politicians can match his ability to energize a crowd. Since his death on October 25, 2002, few national leaders have championed progressive ideals; few have spoken boldly against the rampant greed, injustice, and national arrogance. His voice today is poignantly missed.

But there was also method to his magic. Paul was a talented and careful politician who stood up for his beliefs but did not take unnecessary political risks. He was a skilled, professional organizer who knew how to win. He recognized that it is not enough to inspire people: his genius lay in his ability to turn his supporters into an army of activists and organizers.

Terry Gydesen's photographs help us remember both the magic and the method of Paul Wellstone. In most of her images, he is either moving a crowd to action or holding on to someone while smiling, listening, or persuading. Above all, Terry's pictures depict a man involved in a love affair with humanity. Paul had a passion for people—he loved to listen to their stories and hear about their lives.

Nowhere was this more apparent than at the Minnesota State Fair, his favorite event of the year. Every day for twelve days he would stand for hours in front of his booth (a replica of his famous green bus) happily greeting and talking with each person who stopped by. The lines snaked past the deep-fried cheese curd stand and up the street. He stood there like a host in a receiving line, often touching a hand, an arm, or a shoulder and listening to life stories. With boundless and genuine interest, he heard the joys, problems, and struggles of the people of Minnesota. Paul *loved* the State Fair and often said that the fairgoers were the only focus group he paid attention to. For hundreds of thousands of deeply committed supporters, the love was mutual. Even more remarkable than watching Paul at the State Fair was seeing the people who waited up to two hours in line to thank him for something his office had done, to discuss a position he had taken on an issue, or just to tell him they appreciated his being their voice in Washington.

The pure joy that Paul brought to public life and his utter lack of cynicism also comes through in the photographs. One of his standard speech lines was:

Politics is not about money or power games, or winning for the sake of winning. Politics is about the improvement of people's lives, lessening human suffering, advancing the cause of peace and justice in our country and in the world.

I had become numb to this quotation after hearing it hundreds of times. But reading it now, I see how it perfectly encapsulates Paul's basic philosophy and reminds me of what a unique politician he was. I cannot imagine any other major political leader saying such a thing.

There are great shots in this book from the 1996 campaign. Paul was the target of particularly nasty tactics in that campaign. For months he withstood vicious attacks, distortions, and name calling ("Senator Welfare"). Soft money was backing multiple advertising assaults. Paul was hammered for voting against Clinton's welfare reform bill; he believed the bill would have ultimately hurt children, and he couldn't support it. Pundits expected him to pay for that vote on Election Day. He didn't. His huge support base and his people-based economic message worked, and he won handily. That victory was an enormous moment in our lives. For Paul, it was sweet vindication from critics who said his improbable win in 1990 was merely a fluke.

I will never forget election night in 1996. At 8 P.M. I arrived with Paul, Sheila, and a few others at the hotel room where we would wait out the evening. We turned on the television, and the networks were already calling the race. As we hugged and congratulated each other, I knew this was one of the happiest nights of my life. Paul gave a lot of speeches that election year, but his victory speech that night is one of the most memorable. You can feel the ecstasy of victory in his words as he talks about the triumph of his grassroots campaign:

> And those powerful special interests, they made this race their number one target, but they forgot that I was blessed in being a senator from Minnesota. Minnesotans rejected it, and I have you, and we won this race. They didn't know we'd do literature drops at midnight, they didn't know we'd go door to door, they didn't know about the green bus, they didn't know we'd go neighbor to neighbor, they didn't know we'd go grassroots. We won the race and we did it together!

My favorite photographs are the ones in which Paul is speaking to supporters. Here is Paul Wellstone the organizer. Look closely at these photos: they show an intense, passionate, *fun* man. He understood that excitement and passion, when properly harnessed, can change the world. And that started by moving people— addressing people's idealism and sense of purpose. He brought people to their feet with his words.

Paul won elections because he was better organized than his opponents, but also because he had a winning campaign message. In a television spot that was to begin on the day of the plane crash, he looked directly into the camera and said:

> I don't represent the big oil companies, I don't represent the big pharmaceutical companies, I don't represent the Enrons of this world, but you know what, they already have great representation in Washington. It's the rest of the people that need it. I represent the people of Minnesota.

Wellstone combined this bold, clear message about being on our side with a populist, progressive economic agenda based on what he called "kitchen table issues": decent jobs, health care, good education, and security in retirement. This resonated deeply with our core supporters—voters who want someone who truly represents "the little guy" in Washington.

His economic message came from the stories he heard from regular people. In speeches, he would share what he had learned at the State Fair, coffee shops, and town meetings:

Senator, I'm retired and live on six hundred dollars a month. My prescription drugs cost three hundred dollars . . .

Senator, our daughter has anorexia. She's down to eighty pounds and the insurance companies won't cover it . . .

Senator, I worked for a company for thirty years and now they laid me off and I have no health care coverage . . .

Senator, I'd love to keep working in child care but I can't support myself on the wages they pay . . .

Senator, this farm has been in our families for generations, but with these low prices . . .

Senator, neither major political party seems to care about people like us.

What made Paul extraordinary was that he not only seemed to care about people in these situations but *did* care about them, and Minnesotans recognized this authenticity.

The ultimate key to Paul's success was his large, energized, and organized following. Through relentless hard work, an inspiring and motivating message, and good organizing, he built deep support among many diverse constituencies (farmers, blue-collar workers, environmentalists, communities of color, educators, seniors, students, new immigrant populations) and knit these various groups together into a formidable power base. He never stopped employing strategies that nurtured and enlarged his committed base of supporters.

To run his field-intensive campaigns, Paul surrounded himself with skilled and committed organizers, and it is good to see many of Paul's campaign staff in these pictures. Paul did raise money: in the 2002 election cycle, a record 122,000 donors contributed an average of fifty dollars. Instead of dumping all the money into television ads, he invested in developing organizers who knew how to build the infrastructure required to recruit, train, and effectively utilize tens of thousands of volunteers. This method of organizing also became part of the message. With thousands of people active in his campaign, Paul Wellstone had no trouble establishing himself as the candidate of regular folks, while his opponents looked like the candidates of wealthy donors and corporate special interests.

I know that Terry Gydesen was deeply disappointed that she never made it to the campaign trail with the Wellstones in 2002. I share her disappointment because I am sure she would have made some terrific photographs. It was an exciting campaign, and our organization had never been stronger. Paul was headed for victory, bucking every trend along the way. He was an outspoken progressive running against the hand-picked candidate of Karl Rove and the Bush White House, and he would have won in a year when Democrats were pounded across the country. He boldly stood up for what he believed at a time when Democrats struggled to articulate a message. He mobilized hundreds of thousands of people through his campaign organization while Republicans did better than Democrats on the ground in many states. Paul was close to achieving his third term in the U.S. Senate when he died, twelve days before the election.

What to say about those thirteen days? Terry's photographs show in black and white what I was seeing only through a fog. Thousands of mourners on University Avenue in St. Paul took comfort in each other and left flowers, messages, photographs, and gifts against the chain-link fence outside our campaign office. More than twenty thousand Minnesotans attended a public memorial service at Williams Arena at the University of Minnesota to say farewell and pay tribute in a heartfelt and entirely Wellstonian way. Pain and sadness were palpable everywhere. But during those days I also learned from

Walter Mondale the real meaning of class, grace, and courage. His selfless decision to step in when Paul fell sealed his position as one of Minnesota's great leaders.

Election Day came and went and we didn't win. I felt great sorrow but also a huge sense of relief. The politics was finally over, and it was time to grieve for Paul and Sheila and their daughter Marcia; for talented campaign staffers and friends Mary McEvoy, Tom Lapic, and Will McLaughlin. It was time to grieve for the loss of the joy, the brilliance, and the *potential* of all those people on that plane.

At this writing, more than seven months have passed since the crash, but I still see the familiar green bumper stickers and Wellstone buttons reminding us to "Stand Up, Keep Fighting." Even many lawn signs from the campaign are still standing. Obviously, we're not yet ready to say good-bye to this man and his ideals.

After the accident I received hundreds of letters from people in Minnesota and across the country. One of my favorites was from someone I had never met:

Thank you, thank you for all your work for Wellstone, for Minnesota, and for me!
Thus, I beg you to lift a cudgel and return to the fray, fighting for justice, for the saving

of the earth, for peace, and for the best for the most.

  When the plane went down I donned black, and post-election determined to keep it on until I see any hope on the horizon.

  Being almost seventy I hope yet to see a reawakening of idealism, and so I ask you, implore you and all the Wellstone staff to fight on!!!!!

  For Paul, for all of us.

It seemed as though Paul himself was speaking to me through these words. The guy who would end his speeches to labor groups with the chant "Keep Marching! Keep Fighting!" was imploring me to do just that.

  Inspired by the belief that we can learn from the way Paul practiced politics, and because we believe it is what he would want us to do, the family and friends of Paul and Sheila Wellstone founded an organization called Wellstone Action! Our goal is to teach thousands of people around the country the model that Paul Wellstone employed to win elections and enact political change and to continue the national work of Sheila Wellstone to reduce domestic violence.

  Paul taught me that model twenty years ago, when he was my teacher at Carleton College. I recognized

then that he was an extraordinary person, and I eagerly went to work with him. As his student, I helped him organize farmers in rural Minnesota. As his campaign manager and director of his state office, I applied the organizing skills he had taught me and discovered that they worked. As his friend, I learned the meaning of loyalty and compassion, as well as what it means to live a life consistent with your values.

  I miss Paul and Sheila every day. When I have time to reflect on what their lives meant to me, I sometimes look through Terry's photos. They capture the essence of my friends—people who loved laughing, hugging, smiling, and touching. Paul and Sheila touched so many lives, and these photos show why. But what I love most about Terry's photographs is their depiction of a fast-paced and persistent man of action who was, at his core, passionately and wonderfully alive.

# 1990

Some people are here to fight for the Rockefellers.
I'm here to fight for the little fellers.

**PAUL WELLSTONE**

10

Outside Iron Range campaign rally
**Hibbing, Minnesota**

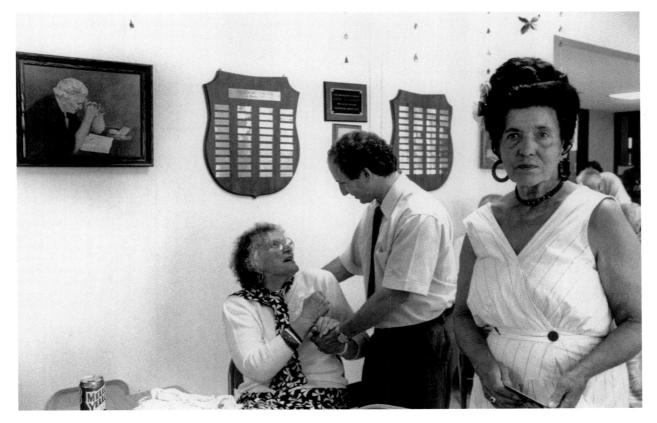

Senior center
**Duluth, Minnesota**

On the street
**Hibbing, Minnesota**

Café
**Hibbing, Minnesota**

Listening
**North Minneapolis**

Hugs
**Hibbing, Minnesota**

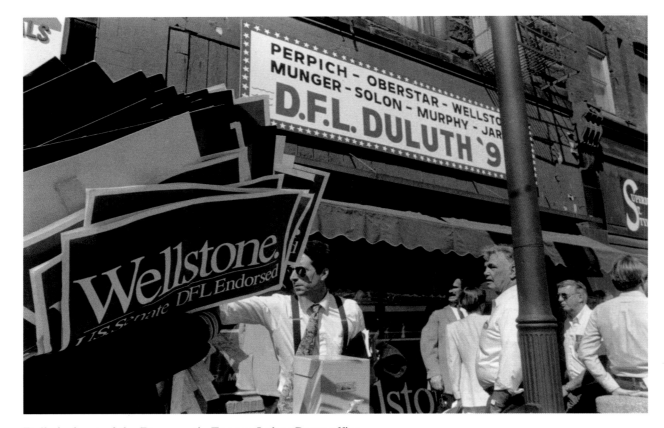

Rally in front of the Democratic-Farmer-Labor Party office
**Duluth**

Campaigning with State Representative Willard Munger
**Duluth**

Paul with campaign manager John Blackshaw on the green bus

Pay phones
**Duluth International Airport**

On the road before the primary with Mark Dayton, then candidate for state auditor
and now U.S. senator

Paul Wellstone and Minnesota Governor Rudy Perpich

Fund-raising call, campaign headquarters
**St. Paul**

Office rally, campaign headquarters
**St. Paul**

Victory speech, election night
**Minneapolis**

Election night celebration
**Minneapolis**

26

Send-off to Washington, Croatian Hall
**South St. Paul**

Marcia, Sheila, and Paul leave for Washington

Arrival in Washington, D.C.

Walter Mondale and Paul Wellstone in front of the U.S. Capitol

# 1996

Politics is not about money or power games,
or winning for the sake of winning.
Politics is about the improvement of people's lives,
lessening human suffering, advancing the cause of peace
and justice in our country and in the world.

**PAUL WELLSTONE**

Paul and Sheila at the Democratic-Farmer-Labor Party state convention
**St. Paul**

Interview at the Democratic-Farmer-Labor Party state convention
**St. Paul**

Paul explaining his position on the Defense of Marriage Act to the GLBT
(Gay, Lesbian, Bisexual, Transgender) caucus, Democratic-Farmer-Labor Party state convention
**St. Paul**

Paul and Sheila greeting delegates, Democratic-Farmer-Labor Party state convention
**St. Paul**

Paul making his way to the stage, Democratic-Farmer-Labor Party state convention
**St. Paul**

Wellstone delegates, Democratic-Farmer-Labor Party state convention
**St. Paul**

Minneapolis Gay Pride Festival
**Loring Park**

Riding shotgun on the green bus

Bus drivers Paul Scott (left) and Dick Miller

Paul and Sheila leaving the Democratic-Farmer-Labor Party state convention
**St. Paul**

Press secretary Linda Marson, aide Mary McEvoy, and Paul work the phones
at the back of the green bus

Paul talks, Sheila rests

44

Side of the road: returning from campaigning in Rochester

Paul and grandson Joshua

Rudy Boschwitz and Paul Wellstone after their first debate at the Minnesota
Chamber of Commerce annual meeting
**Brooklyn Center, Minnesota**

St. Olaf College
**Northfield, Minnesota**

Meeting with campaign manager Jeff Blodgett, campaign headquarters
**St. Paul**

Rallying volunteers at campaign headquarters
**St. Paul**

Back of the bus, Election Day

Paul being interviewed on the way to a rally

Paul and Sheila's entrance at victory party, election night
**St. Paul**

Sheila, Paul, and Marcia arrive at victory party
**St. Paul**

On stage, election night
**St. Paul**

Mary McEvoy and Sheila listen as Paul is interviewed, election night
**St. Paul**

Paul Wellstone was the soul of the Senate.

He was one of the most noble and courageous men I have ever known.

He was a gallant and passionate fighter,

especially for the less fortunate.

I am grateful to have known Paul and Sheila as dear and close friends.

Their deaths are a shattering loss to Minnesota,

to the nation,

and to all who knew and loved them.

**U.S. Senator Tom Daschle**
**October 25, 2002**

# THIRTEEN DAYS

I don't represent the big oil companies,
I don't represent the big pharmaceutical companies,
I don't represent the Enrons of this world,
but you know what, they already have great representation
in Washington. It's the rest of the people that need it.

**PAUL WELLSTONE**
speaking in a campaign advertisement scheduled for broadcast on October 25, 2002

Candlelight vigil at the Minnesota State Capitol
St. Paul, Friday, October 25

Vigil outside campaign headquarters
**St. Paul, Friday, October 25, 3 P.M.**

Jeff Blodgett at campaign headquarters
**St. Paul, Saturday morning, October 26**

Messages outside campaign headquarters
**St. Paul, Sunday, October 27**

Communications director Allison Dobson hugging
Wellstone state director Connie Lewis, campaign headquarters
**St. Paul, Sunday, October 27**

Domestic violence memorial outside campaign headquarters
**St. Paul, Monday, October 28**

Woman at the wall outside campaign headquarters
**St. Paul, Wednesday, October 30**

"I just looked around, he was gone": wall outside campaign headquarters
**St. Paul, Monday, October 28**

Jeff Blodgett on the day of Paul and Sheila's funeral, campaign headquarters
**Monday, October 28**

Memorial service, Williams Arena
**Minneapolis, Tuesday, October 29**

Blodgett family with Wellstone Senate chief of staff Colin McGinnis, memorial service
**Minneapolis, Tuesday, October 29**

Remembering Sheila, memorial service
**Minneapolis, Tuesday, October 29**

Walter Mondale meeting with advisers
**Minneapolis, Wednesday, October 30**

Walter Mondale's nomination for the U.S. Senate
**Minneapolis, Wednesday, October 30**

Mondale lawn signs, campaign headquarters
**St. Paul, Thursday, October 31**

Ted Mondale on the first day of Walter Mondale's campaign, campaign headquarters
**St. Paul, Thursday, October 31**

74

Campaign staff watching Walter Mondale and Norm Coleman debate, campaign headquarters
**St. Paul, Monday, November 4**

Labor rally on eve of election
**St. Paul, Monday, November 4**

Get out the vote phone bank, campaign headquarters
**St. Paul, Tuesday, November 5**

Field organizer Robert Richman in the "War Room," campaign headquarters
**St. Paul, Tuesday, November 5**

Wall of remembrance outside campaign headquarters
**St. Paul, Monday, October 28**

David and Mark Wellstone at Election Day rally
**Peavey Plaza, Minneapolis, Tuesday, November 5**

Wellstone staff, election night
**St. Paul, Tuesday, November 5**

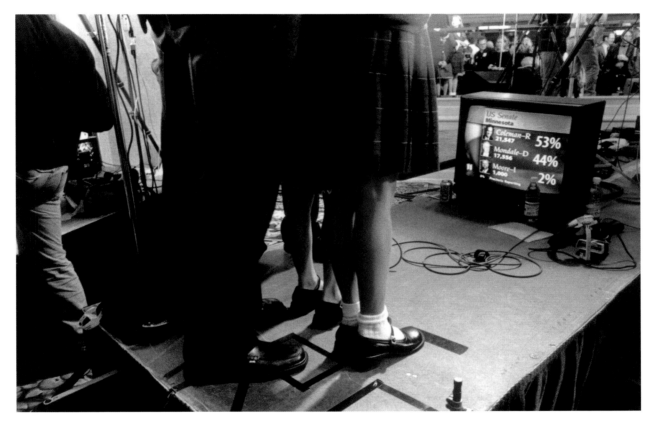

Ted Mondale and his daughters during interview
**St. Paul, Tuesday, November 5**

Wellstone staff after Walter Mondale's concession speech
**St. Paul, Wednesday, November 6**

Hard hat and work boots outside campaign headquarters
**Sunday, October 27**

83

**TERRY GYDESEN** has been a freelance photographer since 1987. In 1988 she was the staff photographer for Jesse Jackson's presidential campaign. She was commissioned by Prince in 1993 to document his European tour, which resulted in the book *The Sacrifice of Victor*. She has received grants and fellowships from the McKnight Foundation, the National Endowment for the Arts, the Minnesota State Arts Board, the Jerome Foundation, and the Minnesota Historical Society, and her photographs have appeared in numerous publications, including the *New York Times*, *Newsweek*, and the *Washington Post*.

**JEFF BLODGETT** met Paul Wellstone as a student at Carleton College. He was the campaign manager for Wellstone's 1996 and 2002 campaigns for the U.S. Senate (as well as manager for part of the 1990 campaign), and he served six years as Senator Wellstone's state director. He now runs Wellstone Action!, an organization focused on training people to be skilled participants in politics and public life.

**WALTER F. MONDALE** served as vice president of the United States from 1977 to 1981 and was the Democratic Party's nominee for president in 1984. He was the U.S. ambassador to Japan from 1993 to 1996 and represented Minnesota in the U.S. Senate from 1964 to 1976. Following the death of Senator Paul Wellstone on October 25, 2002, shortly before Election Day, Mondale ran unsuccessfully to succeed him in the U.S. Senate.